FOXEARTH TREASURES

A Social History of Foxearth & Guide to the Parish Church of Ss.Peter & Paul

Happy Delving !

By Corinne Cox

2014

COSCOX

First published in 2014 by

COSCOX

The Old School House,

School Street,

Foxearth

Sudbury

Suffolk CO10 7JE

ISBN 978-0-9928382-0-1

Printed and bound by The Lavenham Press Ltd, Lavenham, Suffolk CO10 9RN

Contents

ACKNOWLEDGEMENTS

This book would not have been possible without the support of The Heritage Lottery Fund which funded the *'All Our Stories'* project and the excellent support and advice provided by The Media Trust and Access Cambridge Archaeology (ACA). Grateful thanks are also expressed to all those members of the local community who took part in or supported the Foxearth Church Heritage Initiative Project during 2013. Special mention must also be made of the following people who have helped in various ways:

The Graham family, Ken & Margaret Nice, Brian & Annouk Lewes, Nick & Louise Wells (*for allowing test pits to be dug in their gardens!*), David Jackson, Darren Clarke, John Whinney, Malcolm Bonnington, Pat James, the late Gordon(Tom) Hastie (*who would have enjoyed this treasure seeking!*) Andrew Clarke (*Foxearth & District History Website*), Ashley Cooper, Carenza Lewis, Clem Cooper, Michael Wood, Jenny Browne, Gill Morgan, Bill Byford & Nick Hunt (*Lavenham Press*), Janet & Ian Harvey, my parents Harry & Catherine.J.Coe (*for nurturing my love of the past*) and last but certainly not least, my husband Phil Cox (*for putting up with piles of 'treasure' everywhere and being my constant support!*).

INTRODUCTION

"Measure is Treasure" (John Skelton 1530)

This little book aims to reveal some 'hidden gems' of information about the village of Foxearth in N.Essex. It forms part of the 2013 'Foxearth Church Heritage Initiative' (an 'All Our Stories' project funded by the Heritage Lottery) which involved community archaeological test-pit excavations, fieldwalking, archival research and recorded interviews with local residents, in order to help discover, cherish and preserve our local heritage. As a result, many things which had been long forgotten, buried or discarded have now been brought to light and pieces of the jigsaw of Foxearth's past can start to be put together, but the picture is still incomplete. There is still much more 'buried treasure', in the form of people's memories, old personal and public documents as well as clues to the past hidden beneath our feet, waiting to be discovered....so no doubt 'More Foxearth Treasures' will be revealed in the near future!

The reader will find that this book has two parts, the second of which is a short guide to the Parish Church of Ss.Peter & Paul, Foxearth, revealing some of its own hidden gems to the visitor.

"Happy Delving Everyone!" *Corinne Cox 2014*

Fig.1 Artistic view of the centre of the village today

© *G.Morgan*

1. THE FOX'S EARTH.........or is it?

Foxearth is a small village in N.Essex, located close to the southern bank of the River Stour as it changes direction and begins to flow south-eastwards on its journey to enter the North Sea at Harwich.

When we first came to live in the village in 1984 I was intrigued by its name....many reference books interpret the name as meaning *'the burrowing place of the fox',* which seemed somewhat improbable, then a more likely derivation occurred to me. The earliest written record of the village is that shown in the Little

Domesday Survey of 1086/7[1] where it is shown as *Focsearde*. The spelling of the name alters frequently throughout the ages, probably as a result of errors in transcription or simply the fact that whoever was writing or recording at the time was unfamiliar with the dialect spoken and so recorded the name as it was pronounced.

In Old English (the written language of the Anglo-Saxons) there are some letters which do not appear in our modern alphabet: ȝ (*pronounced 'yuh'*), þ (*pronounced 'th'*) and ð (*also pronounced 'th'*). The name *Focsearde* is composed of two Anglo-Saxon words: *'folc'* and *'ȝeard'*. The first means *'people'* and was sometimes used to refer to troops or a fighting force, the second means *'a piece of ploughed land'*.

There are other Anglo-Saxon words, however, which may account for the different spellings of Foxearth in the past and hint at different derivations of the name: *'folc heard'* (the bold, hard or fierce people/troops); *'folc heaþ' (or heað)* (the hard or fierce warrior folk); *'folc earþe' (or earðe)* (the people's or public land); *'folc yrfe'* (the property or heritage of the people); *'folc seofeðe'* (the 7th people or generation). *'folc heahþe'* or *'hearh'* (hill top sanctuary folk[2]).

---

[1] The term 'Little' refers to the relative size of the parchment folio...it is actually more bulky than 'Great Domesday'!

[2] Harrow-on-the-Hill gets its name from this. The word 'temple' equates with sanctuary. Temple End ,Foxearth is on a hill.

Any of the above derivations seem possible when pronounced aloud and viewed alongside the following recorded variations of the name:

1198-1253……………………………………Foxherthe
1202,1232……………………………………Foxherde
1212……………………………………………...Foxhole
1221,1428…………………………………..…Foxhierd.
1246 …………………………………Foxhirde & Foxhierd
1261…………………………………………….Foxerht
1294…………………………………………….Foxeyerde
1314…………………………………………….Foxhide
1362……………………………………………..Foxherne
1363…………………………………………….Foxhorn
1428…………………………………………….Foxzerd
1594…………………………………………….Foxearth[3]

Of course nowadays you can still hear some of the older 'natives' of Foxearth pronounce it as 'Foxuth'!!

So what of the inhabitants of Foxearth before we have written records? We need to look far back in time for evidence that humans were active in the locality, over 400,000 years ago in fact, during the various climatic changes known to us as the Ice Ages

There is much concern at this present time regarding the physical effects of 'Global Warming' and experts believe that we are currently in the middle of what is

---

[3] Examples from Feet of Fines for Essex; Feudal Aids 1899-1970;Red Book of the Exchequer; Calendar of Closed Rolls; Calendar of patent Rolls.

termed an interglacial period. About 435,000 years ago we experienced what became known as the Great Interglacial Period which lasted for some 190,000 years .The sea level was approximately 30 m. higher than it is today. This period is usually referred to as the Middle Palaeolithic[4]. Then some 230,000 years ago the climate cooled rapidly and we experienced what is known as the Penultimate Glaciation (or Ice Age). This period is usually referred to as the Upper Palaeolithic and lasted until 12,000 years ago when the ice finally receded to its current position. The term 'lithic' refers to stone (usually flint) tools shaped by humans. During cold phases of glaciation, the sea level falls and the earth's crust is compressed. In warmer periods, when the ice melts, the sea level rises and the earth's crust gradually expands as the weight of ice lessens. During those warmer periods when the sea level rises, rivers formed from melted glaciers flow slowly to the coast, their flow restricted by the pressure of the higher tides and so deposit sheets of gravel at the new sea level. During colder periods the sea level falls and the rivers are able to flow faster, cutting into the previous gravel deposits and thereby creating terraced banks on each side of the rivers. When this is followed by another warmer period and higher sea levels, these terraces are covered by new layers of gravel and so the pattern continues.

---

[4] This used to be commonly known as the 'Old Stone Age'

Evidence of flints worked and shaped to create tools proves that humans were living on these gravel terraces at various periods of time in the distant past. Dates for the tools and such occupation can be estimated by the heights of the gravel terraces in which they are found.....older tools will be found in the higher levels, as these terraces were deposited earlier and subsequently undercut by river action.

What does this tell us about early inhabitants of Foxearth? Well, as a result of fieldwalking and archaeological test-pit excavations in and around the village, many examples of worked flint tools have been discovered recently, which can be dated to show periods of human activity in Foxearth. The earliest found so far is that of a flint hand axe (probably of the type designated Acheulian) made between 400,000 and 200,000 years ago. It was discovered by Tom Graham (aged 9 years) whilst fieldwalking. It has a yellowish orange patina which indicates that it is from early gravel deposits, reflecting the changing position of the nearby River Stour. Numerous other finely worked flints have been found which date from the Paleolithic to the Neolithic[5] periods. Flint tools, particularly blades, continued to be used well into the Medieval period and beyond. I have often picked up a handy flint to use when without scissors outdoors!

---

[5] Previously known as the 'New Stone Age', a period lasting from circa 4,000 BC – 2,000 BC.

Examples of flint tools, discovered in Foxearth.

Tom's axe and various well worked blades & scrapers

A fine, deeply patinated axe. *(below)*

These early inhabitants of Foxearth have left no discernible traces of their dwellings, some of which would have been temporary shelters or structures reflecting a nomadic way of life, utilising readily available resources and dependent upon climatic conditions. By 2000 BC new settlers had arrived in Britain from the continent bringing and developing the skills of farming, which resulted in more permanent settlements. Such settlements were often located on the fringes of the gravel deposits and fertile alluvial or clay areas created after the ice receded. Foxearth would have been an ideal site. The settlers brought new skills such as pottery making, fabric weaving and metal working and would have, of necessity, constructed more permanent dwellings from easily obtainable materials such as wood. They would have organised a more communal approach to living, for protection against predators (human as well as animal) as they were now farming the land and keeping livestock. Dwellings would probably have been constructed close to each other and simple enclosures created to protect their crops and animals. They would also have begun to bury their dead in some proximity to their settlements. No such burials are currently evident in Foxearth but in 1905, whilst extracting gravel close to Weston Hall (Weston End), workmen discovered a human skull[6]. Excavations in

---

[6] See: Hysterical Historians: Foxearth& District History Soc. Dec.2004.

1907 discovered the remainder of the skeleton which was sent for forensic analysis and declared to be that of an 'Ancient Briton'[7]! Descriptions given at the time as to its position in the ground, seem to suggest that it may be a crouched burial, which was a common practice in the 'Bronze Age' period 2,350 BC – 850 BC. The absence of any grave goods and the position (face down) could also indicate some form of execution burial relating to a different period. Further investigation is obviously needed to verify this identification[8].

Some early pottery sherds found in Foxearth recently seem to date from the Bronze and Iron Age periods but are awaiting validation from a pottery expert. If so, they are evidence of more permanent settlement in the village prior to the Anglo-Saxons.

In the period immediately prior to the invasion of Britain by the Romans (43AD) the climate and temperatures were similar to those of today but between 1000 BC -500 BC the average temperatures dropped by some 2° and there was a long period of cool wet weather which encouraged woodlands to

[7]See 'Notes on a Human Skeleton, found at Foxearth, Essex' by J.M.Wood M.I.C.E. 1907 .The skeleton was presented to the Essex Museum of Natural History, Colchester.
[8] During the late 1980's several small fragments of human bone were shown to me by Heidi Mayhew, a pupil at Foxearth School. These were found in her garden, below the site of the 1905 skeleton.

flourish in our area, providing a plentiful variety of timber to be utilised as the woodlands were cleared for livestock and arable purposes. The writer Strabo[9] described Britain before the Claudian invasion of 43AD in the following manner:

.....Most of the island is flat and overgrown with forests although many of its districts are hilly.......... exported from the island are hides, slaves and dogs that are by nature suited for the chase. The men of Britain are taller than the Celti and not so yellow haired, although their bodies are of a looser build. Their habits are, in part, like those of the Celti but in part more simple and barbaric, so much so that on account of their inexperience, although well supplied with milk, make no cheese. They have extensive gardening or other agricultural pursuits. They have powerful chieftains and for purposes of war use chariots, just as some of the Celti.

The forests are their cities, for they fence in a spacious circular enclosure with trees which they have felled and in that enclosure make huts for themselves and also pen up their cattle, not however with the purpose of storing for a long time.

---

[9] The Greek writer Strabo (64BC – 24AD) made many exploratory journeys throughout the Roman world and published his work 'Strabonius Geographica' in 23AD. The word 'Strabo' was a Roman nickname for someone who had a squint or other eye deformity.

Their weather is more raining than snowing and on those days of clear sky, fog prevails so long a time that throughout a whole day the sun is to be seen of only three or four hours about midday.....

The inhabitants of our locality, at that time, belonged to the Trinovanti tribe. Little proven evidence of their activity within Foxearth has been found so far, with the exception of a bronze coin[10] found in a field near to Red Cottages and dated to the period of the Trinovantian leader Cunobelinus and some possible sherds of Belgic pottery in recent test-pit excavations in Foxearth.

[10] Darren Clarke, David Jackson 2013

Bronze coin of Cunobelin circa 20- 43AD

(dia.12mm)

In May 43AD a Roman force of some 40,000 troops defeated the British tribes in S.E.England. Later that autumn the emperor Claudius and his re-inforcements took hold of the capital of the Trinovantes at Camulodunum (Colchester) and renamed it Colonia. It became a 'retirement' settlement for veteran Roman soldiers. By 47AD all of the south of England was under Roman control and occupation and was formally declared to be a part of the Roman Empire.

The Romans embarked upon a programme of bridge and road building, which would have had an impact on the locality of Foxearth. There was already a shallow river crossing at Rodbridge, on the edge of the village and it is probable that a better bridge would have been constructed. Across the river a Roman fort and subsequent settlement were established in what is now the village of Long Melford. The soldiers stationed at the fort are reputed to have visited Foxearth regularly to obtain pure mineral water from the naturally occurring artesian wells, which would then be transported in large containers, by cart, to the fort. The main Roman road from Colchester to Cambridge, the Via Devana, would have passed close to Foxearth. There are tales, in recent folk memory, of an old Roman road which passed through Temple End towards the Belchamps. Future test pit investigation of the location may well establish if this is the case.

No evidence of dwellings from the Roman period have yet been found, but evidence of a Roman presence has been established by pottery finds during recent test pit excavations in the village[11]and also coins dating to the Roman period.[12]

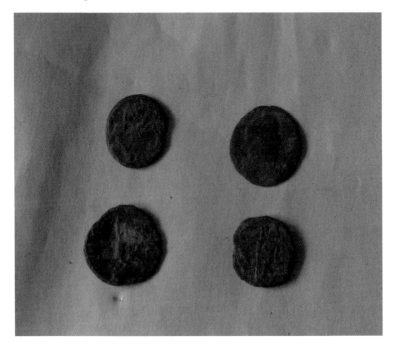

Roman bronze coins :*(top left dia.15mm;right dia.17mm)*

(bottom, left dia.17mm; right dia.15mm)

---

[11] Fx/13 Test Pit 6, ditch fill close to Foxearth Hall meadows.
[12] Darren Clarke , David Jackson 2013

Volunteers working on Test Pit 6 (2013)

(from left: Gill Morgan, Ellie Mead, Graham Brundell, Corinne Cox, Jenny Browne)

(from left: Jenny Browne, Ellie Mead, Phil Cox, Gill Morgan, Geoff Sycamore)

In 61/62 AD the leader of the Iceni tribe, Boudicca,[13] led a successful revolt of neighbouring tribesmen against the Romans and burned most of the Colonia (Colchester) and slaughtered its Roman inhabitants. The rebels continued on to the other main centres of Roman authority, Londinium (London) and Verulamium (St Albans), causing much devastation before they were finally defeated and Boudicca took her own life rather than face capture. The extent of this burning and destruction is still visible today when developers create foundations for new buildings in modern day Colchester and London. All the inhabitants of Foxearth and the surrounding area would have been affected in one way or another by the revolt. Tribesmen who joined the rebellion would have suffered severe retribution from the victorious troops.

There followed a long period of relative stability and general prosperity in the area. More woodland was cleared and agriculture flourished. Crops grown would have included emmer, spelt, six row hulled barley, wheat, rye, wild and cultivated oats, peas flax and linseed. Trade flourished.

By 410AD, however, the last of the Roman troops in Britain had been recalled to defend Rome from

---

[13] The Iceni territory covered all of Norfolk & N.Suffolk. 'Boudicca' was not a personal name but was a term given to a victorious war leader and means 'bringer of victory'.

invading European tribes and Emperor Honorious declared that Britain was no longer a part of the Roman Empire.

The period from 400AD onwards saw many new settlers arrive in our area, travelling from the Essex and Suffolk coast along the River Stour. Some of these were peaceful migrant farmers from the areas such as Denmark, the Friesian Islands and Saxony, who took over abandoned farmsteads and settlements. Others, later, were more aggressive invaders and migrants from areas such as Denmark and Scandinavia who came at first for plunder and later stayed as permanent residents. One of the fields in Foxearth used to be known as 'Dane Pit', we can speculate as to how it got its name! These people were given the generic name 'Anglo-Saxons' and developed farmstead type settlements in the area. No evidence of datable early Anglo-Saxon structures has been found in Foxearth, so far, but the derivation of the name 'Foxearth' suggests their presence.

'Protection money' known as 'Danegeld' was paid to these Scandinavian or 'Viking'[14]invaders for many years and was a source of much local grievance. Between 1012 -1050 an annual tax known as

---

[14] The term 'vik' relates to the narrow estuary settlements found at the base of fjords, from where sea raids took place. Modern day settlements with '-wich' in their name (Ipswich, Norwich etc.) reflect Norse influence

'Heregeld'[15]was levied to pay the standing fleet off the East Anglian coast.

Larger dwellings or 'hals' in which a local chieftain or 'thane' would live, together with his family and retinue of soldiers, would have had a framework of wooden posts, constructed from local timber. These would have had an infill of panels made from a mixture of interwoven hazel sticks and clay, bonded together with straw or animal hair and known as 'wattle and daub'. Sometimes blocks of clay and straw known as 'clay lump' were used, surmounted by a roof made of thatch or wooden shingles. Farmsteads would usually be enclosed or surrounded by simple wooden fences or natural hedging, to protect their livestock. They would contain smaller huts and dwellings for animals, storage and human occupants.[16] This became the model for rural living which was to last until the 19th century.

In Foxearth there is still an area known as 'Claypits' with a Hall and farmstead setting and many properties have been constructed in the village, at various periods of time, using the above materials and methods of construction. In 'Claydens', a cottage at the junction of Huntsmans Lane and Mill Road, there is evidence of 'clay lump' construction in its walls.

---

[15] *'here'* means invading army, *'geld'* means tax in Old English
[16]Reconstructed examples of various types of Anglo-Saxon buildings can be seen at West Stow, near Bury St.Edmunds.

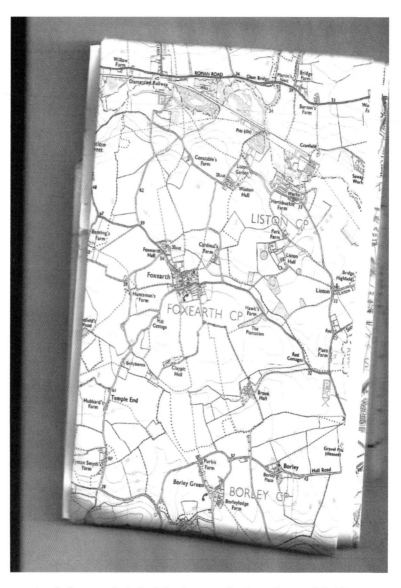

An O.S. map is helpful when exploring the parish !!!

2. THE GREEN BLADE RISES.......

Between 1000 AD and 1300 AD the climate gradually became much warmer than it is today. Vines were grown in southern England and grain crops flourished in East Anglia. The farmsteads in Foxearth would have been comfortably productive during this period, so much so that the village was revealed in the Domesday Survey to be as prosperous as the larger settlement of Halstead. Following the Conquest of 1066 the whole of England was divided and lands given as reward or payments to faithful followers. The new Norman rulers and overlords were keen to have a share in the increasing prosperity of their subjects and the purpose of the survey was to assess how much tax and dues they might levy.

...In Foxearth there are 19 sokemen with $1^{1/2}$ hides and 15 acres. Then, as now, there were 5 ploughs and 10 bordars and 1 slave. There are 22 acres of meadow...

This needs a little explanation. The lands of Foxearth, after the Conquest, had been given to Richard, son of Count Gilbert. He was the 23rd in line in the queue for new land in Essex (the king, obviously had the first pick of choicest land and properties!) following 18 abbots and bishops and 3 other Norman noblemen. There were 88 other recipients after him (including: no.67 Walter the cook, no.72 Roger God-save the ladies, no. 79 Reginald the crossbowman and no.81 Otto the goldsmith. The Saxons didn't get much of a look in….no.80 Gundwin, nos.83 -88 Grim, Wulfgifu, Edward, Thorkil, Stanheard, and finally Godwine.) Anything left over was given to the King's free men.

A 'sokeman' was a free man, a land holder who was not of the nobility but similar to a Saxon 'thane'. He had to attend the local manorial court whenever required by the overlord, to dispense justice (rather like Justices of the Peace or jurors).

A 'hide' was used to assess tax or 'geld' due and was regarded as being the amount of land that would support a household.

A 'plough' was an area of arable land that could be worked by a team of eight oxen (or the value of the resulting crop that it would yield)

A 'bordar' was an Old French term for a wooden hut, hence a cottager of lowly status or 'peasant' owning no land.

A 'slave' was someone who received no income but exchanged work for keep and was not free to leave his 'employment', the lowest person in the social order.

The local administration and jurisdiction of the land was based upon shires[17] which were in turn divided into 'hundreds', usually composed of 100 'hides' or households. This developed into our modern system of 'wards' for local government and 'magistrates' or 'county' courts for justice. We still use the term 'hundred' today.....the parish church of Foxearth is now part of the North Hinckford Team Benefice. In 1086 Foxearth was recorded as being part of the 'Hundred of Hinckford'.

Test-pit excavations in 2013 produced various pottery sherds, which date between 900AD and 1100AD. These are mostly examples of cooking and other domestic wares and help to confirm that Saxons were indeed living in the village during that period.

---

[17] The administrator of each shire being the shire 'reeve' or 'sheriff'.

The earliest building recorded in Foxearth, which is still standing, is the parish church, dedicated to Ss.Peter & Paul. No reference to a pre-existing church was shown in the Domesday Survey. Christianity was first brought to Essex in 654 AD by St Cedd, who was sent to convert the pagan Saxon inhabitants.

The earliest churches were usually constructed from timber and then rebuilt in stone but not all communities could afford such a building or fund their own priest. In such cases priests or monks would travel to villages (early Team Ministry!) bringing a portable shrine and holding the services in the open air (usually close to a water supply for the purpose of baptism) Often the chosen place was marked by a wooden or stone cross. No evidence of any such wooden or stone structure has yet been found in Foxearth.

From 1135 - 1154 AD there was great unrest in the region and most communities would have suffered much hardship during what is known as 'The Anarchy', the civil war brought about by the power struggles for the throne between King Stephen and Queen Matilda[18]. This was also the period which marked the rise in power and influence of the Crusader knights, especially the Knights Templar, who had several interesting connections with Foxearth and the surrounding area. Matilda gave a number of parcels of

---

[18] ..."when Christ & his angels slept"-Anglo-Saxon Chronicle

land to the Templars, including Cressing Temple, near Braintree. By the end of the 12th century they had 'houses' in Sudbury. These were actually small estates, managed in the same way as a manor. The term for a Templar 'house' or *'domus'* was *'Templum'* (perhaps a clue regarding Temple End[19] ?). The Templars were popular with most local people on account of their good works and fair attitude towards their tenants but mostly because Templar tenants, like the Templars themselves, were exempt from various taxes and duties. Such tenants had cross symbols fixed to their houses to mark their exemption. When the Templar order was dissolved after 1314 and most of their lands given to the Knights Hospitallers, it created great resentment amongst the general populace (partly because they were no longer exempt from certain taxes!). There would be repercussions in Foxearth later.

Some of the earliest Templars had connections with, Foxearth. William Marshall (born 1146) 1st Earl of Pembroke had married Isabel de Clare, daughter of Richard de Clare. Elizabeth de Burgh (sister of Gilbert de Clare) owned Foxearth Hall. Richard de Bures (of Weston End) was Grand Master of the Temple 1244-1247. Gilbert de Clare also supported Simon de

---

[19] You can find a 'Temple End' in High Wycombe, Corton Green, nr. Gt.Thurlow, & Weston Colville, all of which have Templar connections.

Montfort's rebellion in 1264. Men from Foxearth would, no doubt, have been involved in this conflict.

Pottery sherds dated from 12th- 13th century have been found in the village, including a fine base of a Hedingham Ware drinking vessel or jug, in the garden of Almond Tree Cottage .

Oysters (below) were a common staple foodstuff of the time

Hedingham Ware: late 12th -14th c. (above)

Oyster shells & Early Medieval pottery (TP 4)

(left)An early 'Guildhall' horseshoe 1250-1270 AD found in a field in Foxearth.

In 1314, Elizabeth de Burgh's brother, Gilbert de Clare, was killed at the battle of Bannockburn. The following year the harvest failed all over the country and the next year 1316, there were outbreaks of 'murrain' (a livestock disease) with many cattle dying. In 1317 there was great famine throughout the land and the poor of Foxearth would have suffered badly. This was followed by widespread drought everywhere from 1321-1325 which resulted in civil unrest with many people abandoning the land and turning to looting and foraging in order to survive. Some of the old manors gained new owners. In Foxearth, Gilbert atte Broke held Brook Hall. Elizabeth de Burgh inherited Foxearth Hall in 1322. William Carbonell held Cardinal's or Carbonell's (Red House Farm) in 1351. Thomas Hunteman held Huntsman's Hall in 1404. In 1327[20] the following are recorded as holding land or property: *Robert de Bures, William atte Broke,*

---

[20] Lay Subsidy Rolls 1327

William de Reppes, John Farmer, Agnes Osemud, Robert son of Edmund Farmer, Simon Osemud, Dennis Freeman, John Newman, William Jordan, Simon Bunting,[21] Martin Carter, John atte Tye, John atte Pole, Sarah Pollard, John de Cristishale (Christ's Hall or Church). These all give us clues as to their occupation or where they lived.[22]

By 1374 some of the fields had been given names: Crabettroufeld (Little Crabtree ,behind Foxearth Hall) Lynersch (Great & Little Lymarsh or flax stubble field, behind the old brewery); Nottynghegh (Great Nutting, a nuttery); Pofeld (Pofield or Goblin's field, a name usually associated with ancient burial sites or pagan rituals, on the road to Pentlow). There is also, around that time, a reference to an entitlement of land at the intriguingly named ' Bellybones', Foxearth.[23] For a long time this house and land, close by Temple End, was known as 'Belle et Bonne', which could be a Norman -French reference to a prime piece of land.[24]

The first recorded Rector of Foxearth is John de Godeslegh, circa 1294. It is not known when the Nave of Foxearth Church was built but circa 1350 the North Aisle was added, as well as the East window in the Chancel.[25] By this time there had been three other

[21] Bunting's Farm Pentlow, perhaps?
[22] 'atte' means ' near or by', 'de' means 'from'.
[23] See Langham Court Rolls
[24] This is currently the home of Pat James, who has created a flourishing natural Wildlife Meadow on this SSSI site.
[25] See Part 2 of this book for more information.

Rectors: Nicholas de Driffield 1310 (brother of Roger de Driffield, the Abbot of Meaux); Henry Bone 1336 and John Botiller 1342

In 1337 Edward III invited Flemish weavers to come to England and many settled in nearby Colchester.We

know that flax was being grown in Foxearth at this time[26] and that flocks of sheep were being reared for the profitable wool trade.

Above: flint loom weight (known as 'hag stone' 19th c.)

Medieval finds: lead spindle whorl, bronze horse pendant, bronze pot leg, bronze belt buckle, lead weight.(D.Clarke)

In 1342 there was a significant rise in sea levels which affected all the East Anglian coast, to be followed by

---

[26] See previous ref. to ' *Lynersh'* or *'Lymarsh'*.

the 'Little Ice Age' which lasted from 1346 -1353[27]. Grain yields fell dramatically and there was a sudden interruption in tree growth.[28] In rural villages like Foxearth news began to spread of a terrible pestilence in Italy, 'The Black Death'.

Shortly before the 'Black Death 'arrived in England in 1348, Richard the Lionheart adopted St George as his own personal patron saint. Prayers made to this saint were felt by many pilgrims to the Holy Land to provide protection against the dreadful plague and so his popularity began to increase amongst the people of England. In Foxearth Church there is a depiction of the saint on the south wall of the Chancel[29]. Although this is a Victorian wall painting, it replicates a common feature of parish churches before the Reformation.

The pestilence reached London in the autumn of 1348 and spread rapidly on account of the wet weather and arrived in East Anglia by the following summer. In September 1349 most of the Suffolk countryside was desolated. As there were fewer labourers left to work the fields, an increase in sheep and textiles developed amongst the villages along the Stour Valley.

---

[27] Experts believe these events were caused by massive volcanic eruptions under the sea.

[28] Evidence from tree rings on timber from the period.

[29] See part 2 of this book for more information.

Because of this shortage of labour the 'Statute of Labourers' was created in 1350 fixing wages to those paid in 1348. In place of multiple field strip holdings, the land was now formed into blocks of 2 acres with a hedge and ditch protection. If you count the number of different varieties of trees and shrubs along a 1m. stretch of any field around Foxearth, you can calculate a probable age for that hedge system…100 years for each different species.

Despite the 'Statute of Labour', wages continued to rise as labourers were scarce. Women began to work as dairymaids or brewers of ale. (Brewing has a long history in Foxearth[30]. The Old School House was a popular alehouse, 'The Fox', for several hundred years before it was purchased by Rev. John Foster in 1850 to become the Curate's House and subsequently the Schoolmaster's House!)

Many yeoman farmers and weavers in East Anglia, at this time, became influenced by the preaching of John Wycliffe and his followers, the Lollards. The English version of the Bible, as opposed to the Latin Vulgate, proved popular with these groups alongside the criticism of clerical wealth and papal power and laid the foundations for future events in the development of Protestantism. Foxearth was to play a prominent role in these events, as we shall see later.

----

[30] See 'Foxearth Brew' by Richard Morris 2004 for more information about the development of the industry.

In 1377 Richard II, with John of Gaunt as Regent, introduced a Poll Tax whereby everyone over the age of 12 years had to pay 1 groat (or 4 pennies). This met with great resistance and proved difficult to collect. 'Serfs' and 'villeins' in East Anglia and elsewhere[31] organised themselves into the 'Great Society'. They had fought in the French Wars and wanted abolition of serfdom and the right to commute feudal service to a payment of 4 pennies per acre. This resulted in the 'Great Rising' of 1381 (sometimes incorrectly referred to as 'The Peasants' Revolt'[32]) and directly involved the inhabitants of Foxearth.

It began in Fobbing (Essex) and then moved on to Brentwood where large numbers of people gathered together and refused to pay the levies needed to finance the wars in France. More supporters joined from surrounding villages and towns and they began to progress northwards to confront and present their demands to landowners, members of Parliament and collectors of the levies. Their leader Wat Tyler and the Men of Essex tended to focus their attention and subsequent attacks on properties associated with John

---

[31] Serfs were technically 'unfree' and could not leave their manor, villeins were 'free' to do so but owed the manorial lords service and labour and had to attend manorial courts when required by their lords.

[32] 'Peasant' was a French term whereby the head of a household was unable to dispose of his property, it had to be passed on to members of the family. In English law a 'villein' could dispose of his property as he chose.

of Gaunt or the Hospitallers (former grievances with regard to the removal of Templars' exemption from dues obviously brought back to mind!).

View of Liston Hall *(shown from land between Claypits & Brook Hall. Hawks Farm & The Plantation are to the left)*

On Wednesday 12th June 1381 the Essex men, led by a priest[33], John Wrawe, were joined by the Vicar of All Saints, Sudbury[34] and more followers and crossed the River Stour at Rodbridge. They mustered their forces at Liston, adjacent to Foxearth. This was a massive assembly of 10,000 - 50,000 men![35] Given the sheer size of the numbers, many of these would have spread out into Foxearth itself. The Manor of Overhall (Liston) belonged to Richard Lyons (a wine merchant, tax collector and financier to the Royal Family) who was not liked, locally. He sat in Parliament as a member for Essex 1379-1380 and did

---

[33] John Wrawe was a native of Sudbury.
[34] Geoffrey Parfray
[35] The number varies according to different accounts!

not do much for his constituents. He was regarded as a corrupt minister of the Crown, keeping some 20% of the dues collected for himself. The rebels were well organised and were comprised of many able, educated and wealthy men who were aggrieved at the state of affairs, as well as poorer members of society.

The rebels wrecked the Hall and burned all the manorial records held by Richard Lyons.[36] They then moved on to Cavendish, via Foxearth, and seized the valuables of Sir John Cavendish (which had been hidden in the church belfry) but did no damage at that time. They returned to Long Melford , encamped close to The Bull Inn and distributed a tun of wine[37] (4,000 pints!) before moving north to Bury St.Edmunds.

Dagger[38]
Pommel

1340 AD

---

[36] Lyons was killed in London on 14th June that year.
[37] Early taverns would hang a pole outside if they served ale or a bush if they served wine.
[38] D.Clarke, D.Jackson 2013.

3. THEY PLOUGHED THE FIELDS …..
……… and scattered the good seed !!!

The diet for most inhabitants of Foxearth throughout the 14[th c] & 15[th c] would include wine, ale, pork and mutton alongside the staples of bread, oysters and vegetable pottage, with beef added by the 16[th c.]   In 1389 a law was passed which forbade the hunting of deer unless of *'a sufficient living'*. This obviously ruled out the poorer classes but was, no doubt, evaded whenever possible. There are still deer roaming around Foxearth (Roe, Red and Muntjac varieties). Fallow deer were introduced much later into enclosed parks, such as that at Liston. In 2013 an interesting find was discovered in test-pit 1 in the 'new' Rectory grounds, a complete antler from a Fallow deer, located in a pit feature. It has not yet been dated accurately but its location near the stable area of the 18th c Rectory suggests it being of that period.

Left: Tom Graham with the Fallow deer antler.

Evidence for a general increase in prosperity for many inhabitants of Foxearth is seen in the construction of new or improved buildings in the village throughout the 15th, 16th & 17th centuries and coincides with the growth and prosperity of woollen towns and markets nearby[39]. All this against a background of rapid change and major events elsewhere such as the French Wars[40], Agincourt, Wars of the Roses, the discovery and opening up of the 'New World' of the Americas. We can only speculate as to how personal lives in Foxearth must have been affected by such events.

There are currently 34 buildings in Foxearth which are listed as being of national importance[41], many of them having been constructed during this particular period. Most are thatched, some have clay tiled roofs and flint or stone cladding and most have a timber framework which helps provide dating evidence.

---

[39] Long Melford, Clare & Cavendish
[40] Commonly known as 'The Hundred Years War'
[41] See: British Listed Buildings and RCHM

In 2013 as part of the FCHI[42] project, members of the community began to research the history of their own homes and some kindly offered their land or gardens for

archaeological test-pit excavation. This has revealed much more information about life in Foxearth in the past.

Top: Orchard Cottage

Above: Volunteers, Alan Border & Jan Lindsey-Smith, TP 3

Left: Ken Nice washing & recording finds in his garden at Orchard Cottage

---

[42] Foxearth Church Heritage Initiative, an 'All Our Stories' community project funded by the Heritage Lottery Fund.

During the period 1350 – 1550 the parish church was improved: the hammer beam roof of the Nave was embellished with angels on the hammers,[43] the North Aisle was widened, new windows with painted & stained glass were provided in the Chancel and on the south wall, the North Aisle roof was painted and the feet of the wall posts were carved with faces or foliate 'woodewose'.[44] Erected between the Chancel and Nave was a roodscreen with painted panels depicting various saints [45] and a piscina created in the south wall of the Chancel.[46] The church benefitted from the patronage of the de Burghs, Thomas Carbonell and William Smyth of Lyston whose will in 1503 included: '..makyng of the Rodeloft of Foxherd'

The Rectors during this period were: Thomas de Hengham(1368), John Wych (?) John Baker (1427), Robert Hathulf (1433/5), Thomas Cordray (1439), Richard Doddington (1485) John Golding (1495) and Robert Mortlack (1527).

---

[43] Restored, gilded & painted by architect Joseph Clark 19thc.

[44] The 'Green Man' fertility symbol, a remnant of earlier beliefs and often to be found in early Medieval churches.

[45] This still exists, though restored in 19th c. See Part 2 of this book for more detail.

[46] The 'piscina' was a cavity, with a drainage hole, in which the priest would wash his hands during the 'lavabo 'section of the Mass and where any water used to clean the chalice and paten, after Communion, would be poured.

Rectors, at that time, commonly had several different 'livings'[47] and services were often taken by assistant priests. John Golding had other 'livings', including those of Halstead and Belchamp St.Paul. He resided at Paul's Hall, Belchamp St Paul and died at Glemsford. His daughter, Margery, was the second wife of John de Vere, Earl of Oxford who entertained Elizabeth I at Hedingham Castle in 1561.

New building innovations were seen in the domestic properties of Foxearth in the 16th c. In place of a 'smoke hole' whereby smoke from a central hearth could escape through the thatch, a large chimney was constructed, using local clay bricks, and often containing hooks or cavities where food could be preserved by means of smoking. Orchard Cottage and Bellybones still have examples of these, along with cavities for keeping salt dry.[48] Not everyone wholly approved of such changes that were occurring throughout the country. In 1577 William Harrison wrote in his 'Description of England':

"Now we have manie chimnies & yet our tenderlings complain of rheums, catarhs & poses. Then, we had none but reredoses & our heads did never ake. For as the smoke in those dayes was supposed to be a sufficient hardening

---

[47] The 'living' was the entitlement to receive rents & dues from the land owned by the church and leased to tenants. It also included 'tithes'(one tenth of the produce in the parish)
[48] Essential for preserving food in warm weather or for long periods. Salt was a valuable commodity in any household.

for the timber of the house, so it was reputed to keepe the
good man & his familie from the quake or pose...."

(from left: **Almond Tree, Peartree, Oakleys Cottages**

As bricks were expensive, however, some houses in Foxearth were forced to retain a simple 'smoke bay' which was a section of the timber roof lined with clay to reduce the risk of sparks setting light to the thatch. Evidence of this can be seen by the presence of soot deposits or burning on roof timbers and rafters. In Foxearth the thatch was of 'long straw' rather than reed, it being more readily available. Echoes of our earlier forebears can be seen in the frequent addition of an up-turned peak on the gable ends of the roof of thatched properties such as Almond Tree Cottage. This is reminiscent of pagan Saxon Y roof finials which invoked the power and protection of 'Odin's frightful horse' 'Yggdrasil.'and was a Runic symbol for the 'world tree'(which in Norse mythology was thought to bind together heaven, earth & hell). The prows of Viking ships depict 'Yggdrasil' as a dragon.

Echoes of this can also be found in the local country superstition of hanging 'hag stones'(loom weights as shown on page 33) over stable doors, to prevent 'hags' (witches) taking horses at night and riding them hard until they broke out in a sweat.[49] Many have been found near the old barns at Almond Tree Cottage.

Above: Y shaped finials on thatched roof

Above: Tudor brick chimneystacks, Peartree & Oakleys Cottages.

---

[49] The origin of 'night mare'.

Towards the end of the 16th c. there was much feuding amongst some of the residents of Foxearth[50]. Some family groups were particularly litigious, such as the Lowe family of Foxearth, the Kent family of Foxearth & Belchamp and the Mayer family of Long Melford,

In 1567 six men from Long Melford and three from Foxearth, armed with pitchforks and pikestaves, broke the bars, locks and chains of a field gate in Foxearth and were fined 12 pennies.

Foxearth Hall Meadows *(view from site of test pit 6 adjacent to medieval or earlier ditch system)*

In 1570, the following were charged with Riotous Assembly: " *John Mayer of Long Melford,(yeoman), George Mowers & Will.Beckam of same (labourers),John Cornwell of Sudbury (joiner), John Lowe of Belchamp Otten (yeoman), Thomas London of Foxherd (labourer) &*

---

[50] Assize Rolls,1578 Brentwood & Chelmsford.

Thomas Lowe of Foxherd (weaver), - for unlawfully & riotously assembling themselves together at the same, for breaking into a parcel of land called Snakeshill & Horsemarsh containing 300 acres (a parcel of land in the possession of Edward Earl of Oxford) & for taking away there certain trees growing there worth 40 shillings belonging to said Earl. And of said John Lowe, Michael Sidaye[51],John Waterynge & John Walker (labourers) & Margaret Lowe (spinster), all of Belchamp Otten, the said Thomas Lowe, Clement Lowe (weavers), Anthony Lowe (labourer),Robert Lowe, Giles Lowe (weavers), Elena Lowe & Anne Lowe (spinsters)[52]& the said Thomas London, all of Foxherd aforesaid for the like and for assaulting Henry Kent & Ann Kent engaged in necessary work there."

The feuding continued….on 27th April 1570 one of the Foxearth labourers assaulted Barbara Kent at Belchamp Walter, wounding her with a dagger, and was fined 12 pennies. The Kents, including Henry Kent of Foxearth, then retaliated by targeting John Mayer & Margaret Lowe. On 23rd June some 20 men from Belchamp Walter, Borley, Liston, Sudbury and Foxearth, including Henry & John Kent (yeomen), entered a 2 acre meadow belonging to John Mayer, mowed the hay, worth 26s.8d, and took it away in two carts. Aided by a yeoman from Castle Hedingham (Tristram Fitch) they then assaulted John Mayer at

---

[51] On a wall of the Cancel in Foxearth Church is a small brass plaque 'Joseph Sidey,gent. Anno 1605' perhaps a relative?

[52] Occupation, not marital status, necessarily.

Belchamp Otten with a *forestebyll* [53]. Their next act was to trample hay, damage hedges, carry away some trees for timber and assault John Lowe's wife, Margaret. They were each fined 6 d. but the feud still continued. In retaliation for the attack on John Lowe's wife, John Mayer stole some of the Kents' horses and sheep. Fields of wheat were destroyed and rustling of animals took place. Tempers began to cool in September when both sides were put under surety to keep the peace by the High Sherriff, Sir Thomas Golding.

We next hear of the Kents in 1578/9 in connection with accusations of witchcraft against Joan Norfolk, Margaret Mills and Margaret Wells, wife of Roger Ganne of Borley. The accusations were regarding *'bewitchment of a grey gelding', 'bewitchment of John Firmin, whereof he died', 'bewitchment of Henry Kent by which for 3 days he was vexed & disquieted in divers parts of his body'.* The women were acquitted but only after Henry Kent the elder & Henry Kent the younger were indicted for assault & battery on Margaret Wells! In 1586 George Clarke (Foxearth Hall) 'locked up' gates, broke down a cartbridge and dug a ditch across the common way which passed through Weston Mill Marsh, Potter's Hill and then towards the church to join the highway leading to London.

The 'Little Ice Age 'of 1550-1700, obviously didn't cool their ardours or tempers very much!

---

[53]An Axe or billhook.

Left: Foxearth Baptism record 1551.

The Church at this time was entering a turbulent time too and the parishioners of Foxearth must have found it difficult to comprehend all the changes of direction with regard to patterns of worship following Henry VIII's break from Rome and the rise of Protestantism during Elizabeth I's reign. Holy Days[54] had been reduced from 90 to 30 days it was ordered that no candles could be lit in front of the altar, there must be free access to a bible (written in English) in each church. The clergy had to teach the Lord's Prayer, the Creed & Ten Commandments in English now, not Latin. A record also had to be kept of all baptisms held in church. In Foxearth the first entry is that of Thomas Lowe, 27th May 1551, son of John Lowe[55].Rectors during this period were Thomas Somerton (1561), Thomas Morse (1595) and John Firmin Senior (1596). The Foxearth Register wasn't compiled until 1558 when Robert Mortlack was obliged to back date entries to 1551. *"Baptizmata…Heer beginnith ye register of ye manner of all those that wert baptized from ye first year of the reign*

---

[54] Labourers were exempt from work on these days as they had to attend church, the origin of our modern holidays.
[55] The same John Lowe involved with the fracas above!

of our Good Ladye Elizabeth, Queene of England. Anno Domini 1559...."

Many of the listed buildings in Foxearth today show evidence of having been constructed or adapted in the 17th c.: Almond Tree Cottage, Claypit Hall with its barn & stable, Burleigh Cottage, Farthings, Cavernash Orchard Cottage, Constable's, Eyston Smyth's ,[56] Foxearth House,[57] Hedgerows, Huntsman's[58], Claydens. Mole End Place, Oak Tree Cottage, Orchard Lane Cottages and Red House Farm[59] Many of these retain interesting internal features, such as mullion windows, inglenook fireplaces, carved beams and panelling. Weston End & Foxearth Hall have moats. The Old School House, originally an alehouse, has one of the earliest intact bread ovens in Essex.

Left: Keyhole shoe 1640 or earlier, found in a field in Foxearth.

---

[56] Formerly Eyston Lodge
[57] A former Rectory
[58] Formerly Hall, now derelict.
[59] Formerly Carbonell's or Cardinals, altered in 17th c.

From 1640-1688 the political and religious turmoil of the Civil War period would have affected Foxearth in many ways. Men would have been called to fight with either the Royalist or Parliamentarian forces, crops, goods and horses would have been commandeered by passing troops. There were local skirmishes in nearby Borley which would have spilled over into the village.

In 2013 several sherds of pottery from the period were found in parts of the village, along with lead shot or musket balls[60] & clay pipes.

Below: clay pipes, 1600 – 1720

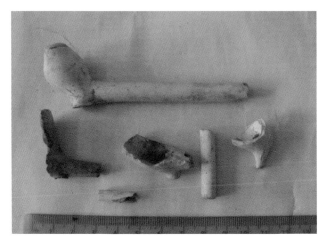

---

[60] Darren Clarke, David Jackson 2013

In 1594, Thomas Morse (Vicar of Boxted) was given the additional living of Foxearth Church. His second wife was Margaret King (by coincidence, the same name as our current Team Rector!) He died and was buried in Foxearth in 1597. His second son, Samuel Morse (b.12th June 1576[61]) became one of the key 'Founding Fathers' of Massachusetts, U.S.A. His direct descendants include: G.H.W.Bush, Calvin Coolidge, Emily Dickinson, James Butler ('Wild Bill Hickock'), Raquel Welch and Richard Nixon!

Religious and political turmoil in England during the first half of the 17th c. resulted in people from East Anglia moving to the Americas in search of a new life. The first group, mainly poor country folk, wanted to break away completely from the Church of England. These became known as the 'Pilgrim Fathers'. Ten years later, a group of local Puritans[62] who wanted to 'purify' the Church of England from within, rather than break away completely, bought the now bankrupt 'Massachusetts Bay Company' and set sail to make a new life in 'New England' on 7th April 1630. Samuel Morse[63], his wife, son Joseph & granddaughter sailed from London on the ship 'The Increase' in 1635.

The Company was successful and by 1640 some 20,000 people were living in the colony. The land was

---

[61] He had a twin sister, Sarah.

[62] Led by John Winthrop of Semer & Groton.

[63] Morse was one of the owners of the company.

divided into 4 counties: Essex, Suffolk, Middlesex & Old Norfolk[64],with towns such as Sudbury, Dedham, Medfield & Haverhill. Samuel Morse, signing the 'Covenant of Dedham', became a freeman & member of First Church[65] at Dedham, Norfolk, Massachusetts. When he died on Dec.2nd 1654 he left over £124[66].

John Firmin became Rector of Foxearth in 1596 and was followed by his son, also John Firmin, in 1638. They are thought to have been a great influence on John Cosin, Bishop of Durham, one of the principal  architects of the '1662 Book of Common Prayer'. John Cosin's father, Giles, (a tailor or 'prick louse') had been born in Foxearth and still had relatives living in the village so John would have heard the Firmins preaching in Foxearth Church. It was during the younger Firmin's incumbency that Foxearth's belfry gained its Miles Graye bell in 1642.

John Firmin (Snr.) held the living of Foxearth for 42 years, his son for 15 years. 'Livings'were indeed for life in many cases, Thomas Cordray (1439) held his for 46 years, John Foster (1845) for 47 years but the

---

[64] They each had 8 towns except Norfolk which had 6.

[65] A 'Congregational' church with no bishops etc.

[66] The 'Morse Monument' 1858, Medfield MA.USA commemorates both Thomas & Samuel.

record must surely go to Thomas Kempe[67] (1653) who held the living of Foxearth for some 52 years!

Left: Two of a peal of eight bells in the belfry.

Following William Butcher (1705) & William Byatt (1730), the first of three members of the Pemberton family (Jeremy) became Rector[68]in 1743. George Everetts (clerk of the church) records the following items as being in the church:

"One silver Cup & Cover marked FP, One Pewter flagon marked Foxearth, One Green Communion Table Cloth, One Damask ditto, One Pewter Plate, One Damask Napkin, Two Surplices, One Master's Hood, One Black Burying Cloth, One Velvet Pulpit Cushion, One large Church Bible, Two large Common Prayer Books, Book of Homilies, Bishop Jewel Works, Erasmus Paraphrases on ye New Testament."

From 1730 the weather became much warmer, the 'Little Ice Age' had ended.

---

[67] He also held the living of Pentlow Church!
[68] The Pembertons, Vicars of Belchamp St.Paul, lived at Pauls Hall, Belchamp St.Paul.

4. A Green and Pleasant Land…..

Not all the residents of Foxearth in the late 18th c. had prospered. 'New Improvements' in farming methods and increasing mechanisation in the 19th c. left many families impoverished, some moved into nearby towns to seek work, some relied upon charity to survive. In 1714 the overseer, William Ellis, recorded the following disbursements for pauper funerals :

"Coffin for Old Snoll -7s; Coffin for Eliz.Edon -7s; Bays -4s; Laying forth -2s; Bell & grave -3s; Affadavit & fetching -1s Minister -1s." and for general poverty:

"For Poulters girls: 2 pair of shoes -5s; 3 yards of ell width cloth for them -3s9d; an apron & sillets[69] -1s2d; Tape binding & woosted[70] -4 ½ d; white tape -1d; 1 yard & ½ ell of molloky[71] - 3s3d; making their coats -6d; for a kettle, frying pan & pottage pot -3s6d; for a hutch, kneading trough & tongs -2s6d."

---

[69] A type of cap or bonnet which covered the back of the neck.
[70] Woollen thread of parallel strands.
[71] A measure, from fingertip to elbow, of a type of soft cloth.

To alleviate the needs of the poor in Foxearth, various charitable trusts were set up by local landowners and churchmen[72]: Bell Rope Meadow (1807, by John Bullock[73] for replacement of bell ropes), Hubbard's Charity (1807, for benefit of the poor), Town Wood (1717, affidavit by John Aldham, Sam Bullock & others, for provision of timber& fuel), Long Meadow (1724, Dr Clopton's Hospital, for the poor). This was followed by Richard Aldham's Charity[74] (1866, for coats & coals) and charities for the provision of 'Sunday Schools' to help educate the poor of the parish. Following the closure of Foxearth Primary School in 1998, a new charity was set up, the Foxearth Church & School Foundation, to support religious & educational purposes within the local community.

The spread of the Non-Conformist Movement in the area resulted in an Independent Chapel[75] being built in Foxearth in 1787. The word 'Dissenter' was often written in the register of the Parish Church alongside the names of those who were absent from a service. There was a growing division between rich and poor.

---

[72] These are still in existence but incorporated into new trust deeds. Payments are still made to those in need in 2014!

[73] Overseer of poor, farmer at Carbonels. Bell Rope Meadow is next to the current sewage works.

[74] The terms of this can be seen in Foxearth Church on a plaque beneath the West window. See part 2 of this book for details.

[75]Used as a garage for many years after its closure, it is now a private house but retains some memorial plaques on its walls.

In 1801, the first National Census[76] was conducted, to be repeated every 10 years. These census returns give us valuable information about the people who lived in Foxearth in the past, their names, dwellings & their occupations, as do various trade directories published in the 19th c. In 1848 'White's'[77] informs us that there were 474 inhabitants & 1,582 acres of land with the main landowners being Richard Lambert (Lord of the Manor), Col.Meyrick, Mr Langdale and Mr Viall. The church had 3 bells and the main occupations were: maltster (Isaac Anderson), straw plait dealer (Fred Bethel), baker/shopkeeper (Dominic Branwhite), cattle dealers (Abraham Chinnery & Edward Upson), corn miller (Elisha Deal), thatcher (Thomas Deal), boarding school keeper (Mary Ince), shoemaker (William Ward), blacksmith (Henry Ives), tailor (George Kidd), bricklayer (James Oakley), parish clerk (Job Ward) & a beer house[78](Joseph Theobald).

In 1863 the landowners were Richard Aldham (Foxearth Hall), Walter Chickall (Carbonels), Henry Coker (The Farm)[79], Margaret Ewer (Old Farm)[80], Edward Gardiner (Lower Hall), Sarah Orbell (Brook Hall). John Foster was Rector & W.H.Irvine Curate.

---

[76] The original purpose was to ascertain how many 'able' men were available to fight in the Napoleonic Wars.
[77] 'White's History, Gazeteer & Directory.'
[78] This is now 'The Old School House'
[79] Claypits Hall
[80] Weston Hall.

There was no longer a tailor or straw plait dealer in the village. The straw plait industry had been set up at the start of the 19[th]c[81] to support the rural poor in our area. Bunches of straw were bleached in sulphur then split down the stem by knife. The bundle was held under the left arm and individual straw 'splints' drawn out by mouth and chewed to make them pliable (no health & safety concerns in those days!).This often led to scarring at the corner of the mouth and was a visible sign of 'poverty'. These were flattened and taken by the dealer to Castle Hedingham, to be sold for the manufacture of straw bonnets & hats in Luton. The best makers could get 3/6d per score and produce 1½ scores per week.[82] The straw was bought from local farms and cost 6d per bundle. Children as young as 3yrs were employed to help but only received 3d per day. The sudden collapse of the industry, due to changing fashions and cheap machine made products, caused hardship once again for many in the village.

In Foxearth in 1863, William Deal now became the brewer & shopkeeper, William Dorling a corn miller, and John Pettit the carpenter. The village also now had a schoolmistress (Sarah Downie), a policeman (James Edward) and a beer retailer (George Ward). Local readers will recognise many of the names above as being those of relatives, ancestors or cottages.

---

[81]By George, 1st Marquis of Buckingham at Gosfield, Halstead.
[82] Rate of pay for a farm worker at the time was 6/- per week.

When John H. Foster became Rector of Foxearth in 1845, there had been seven Rectors since Jeremy Pemberton: John Erskine (1748), John Coulter (1751), John Pemberton (1759), Edward Pemberton (1765), Thomas Wright (1798), Jeremy Pemberton (1810) and Arthur Hugh Pearson (1836). Much has been written about Foster, elsewhere,[83] but suffice it to say that he was a remarkable personality who used his considerable inheritance[84] to restore and renovate the Parish Church, in keeping with Oxford Movement principles, and to promote education by converting the alehouse into a school for children in the village. John Henry Foster was born in Liverpool in 1815. His father, William Henry Foster, was a notable architect in Liverpool and his mother, Margaret Troutbeck, was the daughter of a wealthy merchant[85] in Liverpool. His 1st wife, Rosalind, died in 1848 and the porch in the church was erected in her memory.[86] The tower was renovated in memory of his mother and plaques erected in the Choir to commemorate his father & his son William Henry (jnr), a student of Merton College, Oxford who died whilst visiting Rome, aged 23yrs. Unfortunately, following the completion of some of

---

[83] See 'Foxearth Brew', Richard Morris 2004
[84] £30,000
[85] No doubt linked to the profitable slave trade!
[86] See part 2 of this book for more information.

his restoration work & refurbishment, the 'Colchester Earthquake' occurred at 9.18am on 22nd.April 1884.

The aftershocks of this earthquake[87], which measured 6.9 on the Richter Scale, were felt in the Netherlands, Belgium & France. In Foxearth, cracks appeared in many buildings, including the Church and School House, glass was shattered and many thought that the end of the world was fast approaching!

Below: Foxearth Church in 1830 *(before Foster's renovations. The yews can still be seen but now much increased in size !)*

Foster added a tall steeple[88] to the tower which lasted until 1947, when it came crashing down in a storm.

---

[87] The epicentre was in Wivenhoe, Essex.

[88] There was rivalry with Rev.Bull of Pentlow, as to who could be *'nearer my God to Thee',*so Rev.Bull built Pentlow Tower.

The Church with its steeple *(looking west & south-east)*

As well as embellishing the interior of the Church with murals depicting various saints[89], the rood screen was restored, a new font, lectern & pulpit provided and the crowning glory –a brand new pipe organ installed. This was built & installed in 1862/3 by the renowned 'Father' Henry Willis,[90] at a cost of 300 guineas following Foster's visit to the 'Great Exhibition' in London where Willis's work was displayed. This organ has recently been restored (2014) as a result of local fundraising , grants and a generous donation in memory of a former resident, Brian Prior.

---

[89] See Part 2 of this book for more details.

[90] This organ is listed in the National Pipe Organ Register. Willis was given the epithet 'Father' as a mark of respect for his craftsmanship. He also built the organ in the Royal Albert Hall, the largest instrument in the world at that time.

Interior of the Church *showing murals & organ (far left)*

Below: The 'Father Willis' organ, (now in the Baptistry)

2-manual with 12 speaking stops & 16ft pedal bourdon.

Foster, in partnership with his financier brother, George, helped to develop the brewing industry in Foxearth in 1855 by enabling George Ward to set up what was to become the renowned 'Wards Brewery[91]' in 1855. George Ward was born in 1814 in Western End Cottage. During the 1990s a pupil at Foxearth School[92], who lived in the cottage, wrote in her daily journal about a 'ghostly figure' she often encountered in the house. She described him as an affable man called 'George' with old fashioned working clothes and a big bushy beard. This came as no surprise to her parents who had often sensed a 'presence' in the house. Perhaps it was George Ward, still keeping a watchful eye on villagers!

The brewery prospered and, until its closure in 1963, was the main employer in the village. During test pit excavations in the village many bottles from the brewery were found, several intact (empty, sadly!) from which it is possible to identify the contents & dates of production. Some of these were for beer, some for mineral water which was extracted from the natural artesian wells which are found in many parts of the village. During test pit excavations at Almond Tree Cottage, a layer of natural chalk (the aquifer) was found 20cms below ground level which extends

---

[91]See 'Foxearth Brew' , R. Morris 2004.
[92]Emily Pepper

down for 30-40cms.until reaching London Clay. The site was adjacent to a barn area where several pieces of early to late Medieval pottery sherds were found & included the base of the Hedingham Ware vessel which is illustrated on page 30.

There are still many wells in the village, some with their cast iron pumps intact, as on the former school field, at Glebeside and Claydens. There was also a communal pump outside what is now the Village Hall. The soft, filtered water from these wells was used for drinking, water for washing was taken from nearby ditches or ponds. This caused some health issues, especially behind

Above: Pump handle from ditch[93] Red Cottages where the ditches were a breeding ground for mosquitoes.

---

[93] Found by Rosie Gault & Lauren Christmas, Glebeside, 2013

A solution to some of the public health issues in Foxearth was provided by Ward's Brewery. In 1891 the chalk bedrock was discovered close to the brewery and two large artesian wells were bored, 330 feet deep, to provide a free supply of lime free water for the brewing process. These supplied over 2000 gallons of water per hour! Surplus water was discharged through a series of brick built culverts into a sump area[94]and then through a series of culverts which ran underground to discharge into a ditch system by the Rectory Lodge. Some of this surplus water was allowed to flow into ditches which ran in front of The Old School & School House. Openings made in the

perimeter brick walls, allowed public access to an abundant source of clean water. These 'dipping' places are still evident, known locally as 'pouks' or 'ponks' and many villagers can still recall them being in use as recently as the 1960s. Linda Baker remembers, as a child, catching little minnows in them and Angela Wellman (nee Ham) recalled gathering delicious watercress.

---

[94] Located in the west paddock area of The Chase & behind The Old Forge.

At the close of the 19[th]c, agriculture remained the dominant occupation in Foxearth. Some of the larger land estates were being sold and broken into smaller parcels of land. Many of the cottages were still in multiple occupation but some were now owned by individual families. Boys would find employment as farmworkers, girls would often have to move away from the village and seek employment as servants in farms or the homes of the wealthy elsewhere. Horsemen, wheelwrights and blacksmiths were still much in demand, as farm carts, waggons, carriages & gigs were the general mode of transport. Test pit excavations near to the Rectory, beside the old stables, produced few pieces of domestic pottery but many hand forged cut nails & some cart shackles. Pightle Cottage takes its name from the large cart used to ferry goods to and from Sudbury Market, as well as people!

Mole End was home to the Evans family of village blacksmiths. The smithy was to the left, on the site of Mill Forge & The Chase. The last working blacksmith was Basil Evans, who died in 1984. His father, Samuel was well respected and was Master of Ringers & Steeple Keeper at the church. In 1911 he conducted a peal of Bob Major (5,184 changes!). A board in the church records this feat.

5. FOXHOLES & FOXTROTS ....

During the early 1900s the Brewery continued to flourish and new brick dwellings for the workers were erected as well as new office buildings[95]. There would have been a general sense of optimism in Foxearth at this time. A reading room[96] was set up for the villagers to have access to newspapers, play board games or cards. Electric lighting was supplied from the Brewery. This was all down to the efforts of George Bernard Ward, a lively young man. There were plays and concerts, performed in the School Hall.[97] Whist Drives, gramophone & cinematographic evenings were popular as well as fetes and an annual 'Horkey.

---

[95] Reynard House was the Brewery Office, Magnolia House the manager's home. Glebeside, Pightle Cottage, Bell View & Russets were for Brewery staff.

[96] This later became known as the Working Man's Club & was still operating in the 1970s. It is now a house, Lyttle Hall.

[97] A license granted in 1908 required doors which opened inwards to be taken off their hinges during performances.,

This was a traditional (exuberant) harvest celebration for farmworkers. It was revived at Brook Hall in 1901 by Mr T.Brand for his employees. A local newspaper reported: "*...dinner in the wheat barn at 4pm, meat from the farm & ale from Wards Brewery. 37 sat down with a singing concert afterwards.....a toast 'The King' by Mr John Butcher who led the singing of 'God Save the King'. The health of Mr & Mrs Brand was proposed by Mr Henry Ives, who had lived at Brook Hall since 1865....Mr W.Smith (jnr) proposed a toast to 'Mr Tom & his family', Mr Ellams proposed a toast to 'Mrs Ives, Mrs Deeks, Miss Macro, Miss Byford & Miss Nice' who were responsible for catering....In the concert Mr Butcher sang Fenland songs, Mr Brand sang several 'John Peels'.[98]At 8.30pm the feast concluded.*" A past resident of the village, Reg.Chinnery (b.1910) knew some of the guests who had attended the 'Horkey' and shared his knowledge with the late 'Tom' Hastie.[99] Miss Nice (from Twinstead) was a domestic servant at Brook Hall; John Butcher was a shepherd who lived in the (now) bungalow at Pentlow Street & the father of Percy Butcher; E.Long was coachman at Brook Hall and lived at Hawks Farm; Ambrose Ellams lived at Huntsmans Cottages then moved to a house behind the Chapel; A.Levitt was a gamekeeper who also lived at Huntsmans Cottages;[100]J.Gridley lived at Orchard Cottages; A.Thompson lived at the top of Brook Hall Lane next to Miss Byford; I.Gridley lived at Oakleys

---

[98] A traditional fox hunting song!
[99] 'Hysterical Historians' Jan.20th 2005, Foxearth & District History society website.
[100] This used to be known as 'Lint Growis'

Alfred Deal was the blacksmith at Brook Hall and worked in the smithy by the pond there (he was Eddie Chinnery's grandfather); John Marshall was a mechanic at Brook Hall (repairing binders when they broke down) who lived at Claydens; Henry Ives lived at Brook Hall Cottages (built in 1861, he was the first tenant). Local readers will recognise these names.

There were team sports such as quoits, cricket & football taking place on Church Meadow and an annual outing, by train, to the Brewery Exhibition in London. There were hare coursing competitions at Bradfields Farm & Brook Hall and Coronation & Empire Day celebrations. In 1909 old age pensions were received by men in Foxearth. The village still had its own policeman, the police house being at the bottom of Mill Road. There was a postal office[101] and a bakery & grocery shop. In 1909 the owner, John Robert Wright, was declared bankrupt. He was a former sailor who was also responsible for collecting taxes in the area. His salary for this was £30p.a.but it was reported that "*bad debts, competition & a broken leg led to his downfall*". His debts were a staggering £1000. The business was taken over by Harold Eldred Ham. The Ham family still live in the property, Farthings.

---

[101] The house was demolished but was close to the site of TP6.

Above: Grocery receipt 1911 for Coronation Celebration.

Above: Examples of Wards beer bottles & label.

Bell ringing was still popular, W.P. Gridley rang for over 40 yrs. He rang in the Bob Major on the old peal of bells in 1886. When 2 new bells were added in 1888, he rang in a peal of 10,176 changes in 5hrs 55mins on May 7th! His sons, Percy & Walter also rang the bells.

In 1911, following William James Pressey (1892) and Alfred Marshall (1906), Rev.Harry Stanley Carpenter became Rector of Foxearth. He was well respected in the village and along with George Bernard Ward became an enthusiastic bell ringer (under the tutelage of Sam.Evans).His first curacy had been in the village of Cowley, near Oxford[102]where he used to cycle to visit his parishioners. His frequent punctures were mended in the local cycle shop by the owner's son, Bill, who subsequently became Lord Nuffield of the Morris & MG motor companies! Harry recalled, as a young man, having had conversations with a man who had fought at the battle of Waterloo!

Below: Rev.& Mrs H.S.Carpenter

The pleasures of everyday life in Foxearth were to change when the news of the outbreak of war with Germany arrived in the village in 1914.The 'Great War' was to last for more than 4 years and brought about many changes in Foxearth. Some of the men of the village, who exchanged Foxearth for 'foxholes' in 'Flanders Field' did return home but others were not so fortunate.[103]

---

[102] Information supplied by his grandson, John Whinney.
[103] 'Foxearth Pals', C.Cox soon to be published.

Farm workers from Foxearth were called up to join the A.S.C.[104] on account of their experience with horses & machinery, despite the farmers pleading for their exemption in order to continue to work the land and produce food. As in WWII, women from the village had to provide that labour. Some women, like Ileene Carter[105] joined nursing brigades. Some of the young men who 'volunteered' served in infantry brigades. George Bernard Ward later trained as a pilot & served in the Royal Flying Corps.

The Roll of Honour plaque in the church porch reveals that some Foxearth men were awarded medals for gallantry:

George Bernard Ward was awarded the Military Cross, Frank Chinnery (a stretcher bearer) the Military Medal. *(Above: Robert Chinnery, Frank's grandson).*

At the end of the 'Great War' a tall cross was erected in the churchyard, in front of the Porch, to commemorate those who had served in the conflict. In memory of G.B.Ward, the Village Hall was built.

---

[104] Army Service Corps. responsible for transport & supplies.
[105] She was the twin daughter of Mr Carter, a brewery manager at Wards, who lived in Magnolia House.

In the period between the two World Wars, new houses, provided by the Rural District Council, were built to replace older, derelict cottages in the village which were demolished. The Brewery flourished, as did the shop & post office. The Village Hall was a popular venue for whist drives, concerts & stage plays, a fitting tribute to the memory of G.B.Ward. There was still no piped water supply, this only came to the village in the 1960s. During WWII the village hall was the hub of the village. Regular dances were held, with many parents sending their children to stay overnight in the School House whilst they partied !

Above: Evacuees billeted in the village swell pupil numbers!

School Dinners were introduced & served in the Air Raid Shelter, located on the rear playground. In 1965 this was filled in but its outline is still visible. In 1946 a party for the children was held in the Village Hall.

Above: V.E.Day Party in the Village Hall (chairs still in use!)

Below: Still partying in the Hall 30 yrs later!

Unlike WWI, all the villagers had direct experience of the effects of war, at first hand. Enemy planes often flew overhead, targeting nearby airfields, there were prisoners of war in camps close to the village working in the fields. There were direct hits & near misses. A bomb dropped in a field near Bellybones and exploded, with shrapnel travelling through the front door, through an overcoat hanging on the door and then straight through the opposite wall of the house! A 'Mosquito' plane coming in to land at the US base in Sudbury, crashed in a field near Brook Hall, killing the crew. Local farmworker, Leslie Mayhew & POW Bruno Cornazzani tried but were unable to save the crew.[106] George Chambers was a member of the Home Guard killed in an explosion at Gestingthorpe. The Rector at this time was Rev G.H.Basset who also served in the Home Guard. Pieces of shrapnel are often found when field walking in the village and a recent find in test-pit 1 was a tin of engine 'Gunk'!

Many changes have taken place in Foxearth over the last 50 years and more nuggets of information about life in the village are constantly being collected. The biggest change has been the loss of those villagers who were 'born & bred' in 'Foxuth' but 'incomers' also have their 'treasures' to share for posterity. It is heartening to see so many young people in the village developing a curiosity about life in the past. They are

---

[106] A plaque in the church porch commemorates this event.

the 'treasure' seekers of the future! 'More Foxearth Treasures' will no doubt soon be in production!

This collection of 'gems' began with the village sign and so it is appropriate to end with it. Renovated a little while ago by the Parish Council of Foxearth & Liston, it was originally the gift of a local farming family, the Chapmans, in memory of their time at Foxearth Hall. The picture below is of its unveiling. Many of the people present still live in Foxearth but some are no longer with us. Local readers will no doubt recognise many faces!

Part 2

TEXTS & IMAGERY IN THE PARISH CHURCH OF Ss PETER & PAUL FOXEARTH

There has been a parish church in the village of Foxearth for over 800 years, during which time many changes have been made to the fabric and to the decorations and embellishments both within and outside the building. Time and the elements have not always treated the building kindly and there is a real danger that many of the decorative effects in the church may soon be lost forever. With this in mind I have produced the following guide to help visitors to the church locate, decipher and appreciate the many and varied texts and images found here.

Corinne Cox

Fig. The South Porch, Ss.Peter & Paul, Foxearth

© J.Browne

THE TOWER:

As you approach the tower from the north (the new churchyard) you will notice that three sides have clock faces with limestone carvings and sculptures adjoining each quarter of the faces. The north face is decorated with various types of flowers and foliage, representing the 3rd day of Creation " *Let the earth produce all kinds of plants" Gen.1.11.*

The west face shows two birds in a fruit tree, two birds sitting on a nest, two birds pecking amongst ears of wheat and three birds in a holly tree with berries, representing not only the four seasons but the 5th day of Creation *"Let the air be filled with birds…he told the birds to increase in number" Gen.1.20,22.*

The south face shows a lamb, a rabbit, a squirrel and a fox, representing the 6th day of Creation *"Let the earth produce all kinds of animal life: domestic and wild, large and small" Gen.1.26.*

Beneath the clock faces, from north to south, inscribed in red lettering on sandstone, is the following dedication to Rev.J.Foster's mother:

This tower was built in the year of our Lord 1862 to the Glory of God Father Son and Holy Ghost and to the pious memory of Margaret Foster who deceased Easter Eve 1861.

THE PORCH:

From the left of the Porch to the right there is the following dedication carved in relief in sandstone:

+ Precious in the sight of the Lord is the death of his saints   R F.

Continuing over the main arch of the entrance to the porch, inscribed in black on sandstone:

Bless Gods Holy Name for his servant Rosalind Foster who departed this life in his faith and fear".

The remainder of the inscription, carved in sandstone (for Foster's 1st wife) continues:

+Be not slothful but followers of those who through faith and patience inherit the promise RF.

Inside the porch you will see windows on the right and left, each comprised of two painted glass panels:
Left: (a) Noah and the Ark,
(b) Moses leading his people and the parting of the Red Sea. Notice the inclusion of St.Christopher and the Christ Child in the bottom left hand corner…both appropriate images for worshippers journeying to church!
Right: (a) Christ preaching to children & adults.
(b) Baptism of Christ by John the Baptist.

The imagery in these panels reflects the traditional role of the porch as that part of the church in which preaching, baptism & weddings took place in the past.

Above the window on the left is an inscription, in sandstone: *Built by John Foster M.A. Clerk, Rector of this parish in the year of our Lord God 1848.*

To the right of this window are two brass memorial plaques, the top one is dedicated to the Men of Foxearth who served their country by land, sea & air in the 1st World War 1914-1919 and lists their names. Notice that Nurse Ileene Carter, whose name appears on the memorial cross outside the church and whose grave is to the right of the porch, is not included!

The lower plaque commemorates:

Flt.Lt Edward Gary Sheppard, Pilot Age 25 and Flt.Sgt. Fred. George Ward, Navigator, Age 20 R.A.F. who lost their lives near Brook Hall Foxearth on 6th March 1945, in defence of this country & to remember Leslie Mayhew and Bruno Cornazzani (POW) who also risked their lives to help them.

In the archway above the elaborately carved oak **main door**, in red and black paint, is the following inscription:
This is none other but the house of God and this is the gate of heaven.

BAPTISTRY:

The famous Father Willis **organ** is currently sited immediately in front of the original Baptistry at the west end of the church. It is a beautiful instrument with much gilding on its case and pipes. It was restored in 2014. On the front panels you can see, from left to right: a vase with lilies and inscribed ribbon banner – *Non dox sed votum, Non musica chorda sed cor ;* an angel playing an early organ; an angel playing a viol; an angel playing an early trumpet; a vase with Tudor roses and inscribed ribbon banner – *Non clamans sed amans Psallit in aure Dei (all sounds & music freely given from the heart are but songs of praise in God's ears).*

Behind the organ is the **Baptistry.** It originally housed the stone font which is now in the North Aisle

The **West Window** is divided into 4 large panels beneath smaller ones, which depict aspects of the Resurrection and acts of healing & charity:

(a) the sponge, spear & crown of thorns; angels at the empty tomb; Jesus healing the blind man

(b) the women at the tomb; the raising of Lazarus;

(c) the Pyx of Veronica (cloth used to wipe Jesus' face on way to Calvary); figure of Christ with banner; Jesus healing the cripple;

(d) the women at the tomb with ointments; healing of Jairus' daughter.

Below this window is a rectangular brass plaque describing the terms of the **Aldham Charity:**

Richard Aldham who died at Foxearth Hall on March 8 AD 1866 by his will left to the Rector & Churchwardens of the parish of Foxearth the sum of 600 pounds upon trust to apply the interest of 100 pounds towards the Sunday Church School and to apply one moiety of the residue of such interest in purchasing a great coat each for 6 of the eldest men and a cloak each for 6 of the oldest women living in and belonging to the said parish of Foxearth. Such men and such women the recipients having been respectively constant attendants at the services of the parish church. The said coats & cloaks to be given to the said men and women alternately every year on the 28th day of November and to apply the other remaining moiety for purchasing coals to be given away or sold at a reduced price during the winter season every year to the poor belonging to and living in the said parish of Foxearth.

NAVE:

Stand in front of the organ and look up at the beams in the Nave towards the Chancel. These are all ornately painted with patterns and the following texts from the 'Te Deum':

(a)To Thee all angels cry aloud the heaven and all the powers therein

(b) All the earth doth worship Thee the Father Everlasting

(c) We praise Thee God we acknowledge Thee to be the Lord

(d) Thou art the King of Glory O Christ, Thou art the everlasting Son of the Father

Prior to 1965 all the walls were highly decorated with painted biblical scenes but in an attempt to increase light inside the church these were covered by whitewash. If you look closely above the arch nearest to the lectern you can just distinguish the outline of the **Arms of the Holy Trinity,** a shield with circles in each corner which would have borne the words: *Pater, Filius, Spiritus Sanctus (Father, Son, Holy Spirit)* linked to each other with the words: *non est (is not)* and linked to a central circle containing the word *Deus (God)* by the word *est (is)*

Above the **Rood Screen** is a large semi-circular painting depicting Christ in Majesty. Look at Christ's feet, beneath them is a sphere which usually represents the World but if you look carefully inside the sphere you will see that the artist has painted Foxearth Church. The view is taken from the fields to the north of the church and shows the church as it looked in 1868, following Foster's renovations, with the tower surmounted by a steeple.

This steeple was destroyed by a storm in 1947.The rooftops of Foxearth Hall are visible in the right corner of the picture.

Surrounding the figure of Christ are various angels and also four winged figures with texts from the 'Te Deum', representing the Four Evangelists Ss.Matthew, Mark, Luke & John who are also identified as the Four Beasts who surround the

Throne in the Book of Revelations. Their images were assigned from the opening verses of their own gospels :

(a) Lion (Resurrection): St.Mark *(a voice crying in the wilderness, the lion)* **I know that my redeemer liveth**

(b) Man (Humanity): St.Matthew *(Jesus' lineage born of woman)* **O Lord save thy people & bless thine inheritance**

(c) Eagle (Divinity): St.John *(eagle soaring to the sun)* **O Lord have mercy upon us**

(d) Ox (Sacrifice):   St.Luke *(sacrifice offered by Zachariah)* **O Lord in thee have I trusted never let me be confounded**

If you look up at the roof beams of the Nave facing towards the organ, you will see a continuation of the earlier decorations and texts:

Heaven and earth are full of the majesty of thy glory

Holy,Holy, Holy Lord God of Sabaoth

To Thee Cherabim and Seraphim continually do cry

The **Rood Screen** is so named because the screen or partition which traditionally separated the Nave from Chancel is surmounted by a large crucifix (the word *rood* comes from the Anglo-Saxon, meaning *that which is raised up)*. In this church the **Rood** is particularly fine and the carved figure of Christ on the Cross is flanked by Mary and John. Beneath the figures is the carved text *: Behold the lamb of God which taketh away the sins of the world St.John1.29*

Below this, running along the screen are carvings of foxes chasing bunches of grapes, a reference to the devil or Satan trying to steal the blood of Christ.

Along the base of the rood screen are a series of **painted panels** depicting a variety of saints with their names, symbols & attributes. Female saints are shown on the left of the chancel gates, males on the right, a pattern which continues through the Chancel.

 The symbols & attributes associated with each saint or martyr usually depict an aspect of their life or death. Martyrs are also usually given the symbol of a palm leaf. In medieval times prayers were often dedicated to particular saints who it was felt may have a particular affinity with individual problems.

(a) St.Barbara, (tower) – imprisoned in a tall tower by her father and tortured. As he cut off her head he was struck by lightning. Patron saint for protection against lightning.

(b) St.Helena (cross) –mother of the Emperor
Constantine, reputedly found Christ's cross
(c) St.Mary Magdalene (pot of ointment) - patron
saint of penitents
(d) St.Dorothy (fruit & flowers) – protector from
storms, fire & sudden death
(e) St.Appollonia (pincers) – tortured by having
teeth pulled out, patron saint of teeth
(f) Blessed Virgin Mary (crowned as Queen of
Heaven) patron saint of mothers
(g) Christ in Majesty (I H S) – Jesu Hominum
Salvator (Jesus Saviour of Mankind)
(h) St.Alban (sword) – Britain's first martyr.
(i) St.Walstan (scythe) – patron saint of farm
workers, local saint.
(j) St.Felix (anchor) - local saint
(k) St.Edmund (arrow) king of E.Anglia murdered
by Danes, local saint.
(m) St.Augustine (heart) –patron saint of brewers

LECTERN:

The purpose of the Lectern is to hold the large
church Bible. This one is skillfully carved and takes
the form of an eagle holding a ribbon in its beak
which flows back under its wings and is inscribed:

*If any man shall add unto or take away from the words
of this book God shall take away his part out of the book
of life*

Its feet stand on a sphere surrounded by emblems of
the Four Evangelists with the text:

Holy Holy Holy Lord God Almighty which was and is and is to come Amen

Beneath is a tower supported by pillars and the text:
The church built upon the foundation of the apostles, prophets, Jesus Christ himself the first corner stone

PULPIT:

Painted panels around the pulpit depict the Fathers of the Church: **St.Gregory** (altar & chalice); **St.Augustine** (heart); **Christ, King in Majesty**; **St Ambrose** (scourge); **St.Jerome** (lion)

CHANCEL:

Around the walls from left to right are wall paintings depicting saints and martyrs with their symbols & attributes, above the following text:

O Almighty God grant us grace so to follow thy blessed saints in all virtuous and godly living that we may come to those unspeakable joys which thou hast prepared for them that unfeigningly love thee, through Jesus Christ our Lord Amen.
St.Cecilia ,Virgin Martyr(organ/harp); **St.Prisca VM** (lion & sword); **St.Agatha VM** (dish, jug & shears); **St.Agnes VM** (sword); **Aethelreda Queen & Abbess; St Lucy VM** (pincers,cauldron,sword); **St Osyth** (stag); **St Athelburga Queen**; **St Elizabeth** (jug); **St.Perpetua** (cow); **St Margaret** (lance & dragon); **St Rosalie** (distaff); **St Ann** (fruit);

St **Catherine** (wheel); St **Helen** (cross); St **Mary Cleophas** (jug); **Blessed Virgin Mary** (keys); St **Mary Magdalene** (box of ointment).
St **Paul, Apostle** (sword & book); St **Peter, Apostle** (keys & scroll); St **Boniface** (scourge & spear); St **David; Venerable Bede** (book); St **Lawrence** (gridiron); St **Benedict,** Abbot (rods); St **George** (dragon); St **Alban** (sword); St **Edward the Confessor** (crown & ring); St **Crispin** (awl); St **Edmund** (arrow); St **William of Norwich** (nails)

The **Choir Stalls** on each side of the Chancel have elaborately carved foliate ends, known as Poppy Heads, each with a different design. The arms also have carvings of individual figures:

Front Left: Clerk; Man with book; **Angel**; Woman with scroll; **King** at prayer with text: *Christ have Mercy*
Back Left: Clerk with closed book; **Clerk** with open book; **Clerk** with closed scroll.
Front Right: Clerk at prayer; **Angel** with hands on breast; **Angel** with scroll; **Angel** with hands down with text: *Lord have Mercy*
Back Right: Nun with wimple; **Bearded man** with open book; **Priest** with open scroll.

The **Priest's Stall,** on the right behind the Rood Screen, has the following carved text:
O Christ hear us, O Lord help us, Lord have mercy upon us

On the wall immediately behind this are two brass plaques, the top one is mounted on polished black slate and bears the inscription:

In every work that he begat he did it with all his heart and prospered. William Henry Foster BA of Merton College Oxford fell asleep at Rome May 11th 1868 aged twenty three years. Grant O Lord that he may rest in peace. Amen.

The lower plaque is of brass :

Jesus + Mercy In loving memory of John Foster, Priest 46 years Rector of this Parish who fell asleep at Foxearth March 18th 1892 aged seventy seven years. Make them to be numbered with thy saints in Glory everlasting.

Below the **South Window** in the Chancel is a brass inscription:

To the Glory of God the Father Son and Holy Ghost and in the pious memory of William Foster of Liverpool Esquire born January 11th AD MDCCLXXXVIII (1788) Died May 6th AD MDXXCXXVI The windows of this chancel are dedicated by his wife and surviving children.

On the **North Wall** of the Chancel is a small brass plaque hinting at a possible crypt below:

Joseph Sidey Gent. Lyeth heare buryed who died the XI day of June Anno 1605

The **East Window** above the altar has three panels of stained and painted glass with texts:

Top: *I.H.S.*

Left: *He that believeth and is baptized shall be saved*

(image of Christ preaching)
 Centre: *God so loved the world that he gave his only begotten son to the end that all that believe in him should not perish.*
 (images of Christ carrying his cross, Christ crucified, Christ placed in tomb in his shroud)
 Right: *Who so eateth my flesh and drinketh my blood hath eternal life and I will lift him up at the last day.*
(image of the Last Supper).

ALTAR:

The Altar table has a finely carved and gilded reredos, which has six panels.

From Left to Right : **Noah** giving thanks with the Ark safely on Mt.Ararat; **Abraham** about to sacrifice Isaac; **Agnus Dei**, the sacrificial Lamb of God standing on an altar; **Judaic** rite of priestly sacrifice with burnt offerings of ox and ram (Leviiticus); **Altar of Incense**, the rite of priestly prayer; the **Altar of Witness** ,stones from the River Jordan (Joshua).

Beneath this is a plinth carved with vines and the text: *Very God, Jesus the light of the world, Very God.*

Below the altar table are a panels of fine paintings depicting: **The Annunciation, Birth of Christ, Last Supper, Christ in the Garden of Gethsemene, Christ being taken down from the Cross.**

On the wall behind the altar are painted panels depicting: **Ss.Jude, Simon, Bartholomew, James the Less, James, Thomas, David ,Matthew and Matthias**.

The **Altar Gates** are flanked by two identical carved wooden angels, one bearing the text: *Holy, Holy, Holy* and one bearing the text: *Lord God of Hosts.*

 Below the rails are carved emblems of Christ's Passion: *pillar, crossed scourges, crown of thorns, crucifix, INRI, hammer, 3 nails, sponge on stick, spear, ladder, pincers.*

VESTRY:

This was originally the **Lady Chapel** and at one time also housed the organ. You can see the open tracery panels behind the curtain and the brass holder for the oil lamp. If you look carefully on the side of the carved door leading into the Chancel you will find the carpenter's name: *Ben Cooper .Clare*

The **North Window** has three panels with dedications beneath each: **St.Anne , St.Mary Magdalene, St.Margaret** :

 To the Glory of God & in memory of three sisters Anne Foster died xvi October MDCCCXXXVI Aged XX years, Mary Duncan died XIX July MDCCCXXII Aged19 years, Isobel Margaret Foster died XIX MDCCCXXXXVI Aged 16 years.

The **East Window** also has three panels but the faces of the female figures in each are obliterated. The dedication below it is:

To the Glory of God in memory of his servant Rosalind wife of John Foster MA Clerk & Rector of this parish departed this life January III.

NORTH AISLE:

Look up at the beams again and you will find the following texts:

Enter not into judgement with thy servant Lord +
This is the law of the prophets +
If ye love me keep my commandments +
No man can serve two masters God and Mammon +

On the bases of the beams you will see simple carved and painted faces which are much older than other decorations in the church and date to 14th c.

The West Window shows various heraldic crests and coats of arms, including those of the Foster families.

In front of the window is the octagonal stone **Font**. Carved into each side panel you can see:
IHS, Dove, Angel (St Matthew ,book), Agnus Dei (Lamb of God), **Winged Lion** with scroll (**St Mark**), **Winged Ox** with scroll (**St Luke**), **Star of David.**
The font cover is finely carved, surmounted by a **Pelican** pecking at its breast, symbolizing Christ shedding his own blood to redeem mankind. The cover is raised by a pulley & elaborate carved weight.

The South Windows in the Nave are each divided into three panels with three scenes in each panel:
(a) **Elijah** being fed by ravens; **Elijah**; **Elijah** in the fiery chariot.
(b) Blank pane
(c) **Noah** building the ark; **Noah**; **Noah** sacrificing a lamb on an altar (JF MDCCCI iv)
(d) **Joseph** recounting his dream of sheaves**; Joseph** sold in slavery; **Joseph**'s brothers paying tribute to him in Egypt.
(e) Blank pane.
(f) **David** being anointed; **Priest** with the Ark of the Covenant; **King David** and his harp.

On leaving the church notice the **Table of Kindred and Affinity** on the main door. In most small knit communities in the past, it was important to ensure that the congregation was aware of any "known impediment" to an intended marriage.

The **Offertory Box** has been relocated from its original position. You can still see the text written on the back of the first pew where it was originally fixed

He that hath pity on the poor lendeth unto the Lord and look what he layeth out it shall be paid him again +

Pause to look above the gated entrance to the church where you will see another text painted around the archway:

Remember all thou hast received and how and hold fast and repent.

THE LYCH GATE:

As you leave the churchyard pause by the lych gate.
Its original purpose was to provide a temporary
resting place for a coffin prior to burial (*lycche* in
medieval times meant 'body').
Above the tiles on its roof you will see an iron cross
and below that a wooden carving of Christ resting
whilst carrying his cross to Calvary. Look up inside
the gate and you will discover another text:

*This lychgate was restored and dedicated on 11th
November 1966 to the Glory of God and in loving
memory of Lieut.Thomas Harvey Overbury Capron 1/5th
Essex Reg. Killed at Gaza 26th March 1917 aged 21.*

Fig.3   The Lych Gate in winter   © J.Browne